ENCHANTING AND POTIONS HANDBOOK FOR MINECRAFT

MASTER THE ART OF ENCHANTING IN MINECRAFT

UNOFFICIAL MINECRAFT GUIDE

BlockBoy

Disclaimer

All Rights Reserved. Any content of this publication cannot be replicated or transmitted by any means or in any form including electronic, print, photocopying, recording or scanning without any written consent from the publication's author.

The author has tried to be an authentic source of the information provided in this report. However, the author does not oppose the additional information available over the internet in an updated form. The objective of providing different secrets of Minecraft to the players is to help them play to their best. The Minecraft secrets included in this book cannot be compared with the guidelines provided with other books. All readers can seek help from game experts for further advice.

Ignoring any of the guidelines or not following the game instructions may lead to getting low scores in the game. Therefore, the author is not responsible for such negligence.

Table of Contents

About This Guide...5

Brewing Prerequisites 7

   Brewing Stand 8

   Ingredients...10

Potions...17

   Awkward Potion.................................... 17

   Potion of Swiftness 18

   Potion of Strength 19

   Potion of Healing.................................. 20

   Potion of Regeneration 21

   Potion of Fire Resistance...................... 21

   Potion of Night Vision.......................... 22

   Potion of Invisibility............................ 23

   Potion of Water Breathing 23

   Potion of Weakness 24

   Potion of Poison................................... 25

   Potion of Slowness 25

   Potion of Harming 26

Enchanting...27

   Enchanting and Anvils 32

   List of Enchantments........................... 32

Conclusion 36

About This Guide

Minecraft is a sandbox game originally developed by Swedish video game programmer Markus 'Notch' Persson. The game was inspired by other, older, classic games like Dwarf Fortress, Dungeon Keeper and Infinminer. At its very basic level, Minecraft is a building game. However over time elements of Survival game play have also been added which has led to Minecraft's popularity.

Like many other games, the survival game play mainly involves collecting resources and using them to craft items like weapons and armor. But apart from that in Minecraft, you can also use some ingredients to brew potions. Furthermore, while other games let you use accumulated XP to level up and gain abilities, in Minecraft, you can use the XP to enchant your equipment which can give you powerful bonuses.

The purpose of this guide is to help you collect the necessary items required to brew the best potions and ways in which you can make the most out of the enchantments available at your disposal. This guide should help you in better understanding the whole process of brewing potions and enchanting equipment. I hope that you will enjoy reading and using this guide as much as I enjoyed writing it.

This guide was written for Minecraft (PC) version 1.8 and is accurate in the information it provides up to that version.

Brewing Prerequisites

Potion brewing is a rare art. Most people who play Minecraft spend most of their time building and exploring and at the most, crafting the most necessary equipment. Few know the potential that lies locked up in the tiny little glass bottles.

While potions are not very important on lower difficulties, having the correct potion in your inventory is pretty much a requirement on Hard Difficulty, especially if you are preparing to fight a boss mob like the Ender Dragon or the Wither. In such cases, a potion can mean the difference between failure and success.

There is a variety of potions that can be brewed in Minecraft and most of them serve very specific purposes. In the sections below, we will discuss the most useful of these potions - how to brew them, what ingredients will you need to brew them and if the ingredients are rare, notes on how to obtain those ingredients will be provided.

To begin with, there are certain prerequisites that need to be met before you can start brewing and one of these is having the correct equipment at hand. We begin with the most important brewing equipment, the brewing stand.

Brewing Stand

A brewing stand can be crafted using three blocks of cobblestone and one blaze rod. You will, of course, have to venture into the Nether to obtain the blaze rod. Once you have crafted the stand, you need to place it on a solid block to use it.

When you right click on the stand, you will see an interface as shown below. This is the brewing interface. The three slots at the bottom are the slots where the potion bottles go. In the slot on the top, you need to put the ingredient you want to be distilled in the bottles.

This means each unit of ingredient can be distilled into three potions at a time.

Once you have a brewing stand ready to be used, there are several other things you need before you actually start the brewing. You need to get glass bottles. They can be crafted using glass blocks which are obtained by smelting sand.

You also need a source of water from where to fill the bottles. A simple infinite water block next to the brewing stand is a good idea. Or if you want to role play and do stuff by the book, you can also use a cauldron which you can then refill with a bucket.

Last but not the least, you will need Netherwarts. More on this in the next section.

Ingredients

Below is a list of the most important ingredients that are required to brew the potions, along with a brief summary about their uses, where to find them and how. If you are serious about brewing, it is a good habit to stockpile these ingredients in separate marked chests so that you can get a brewing whenever you want.

1. Blaze Powder

Blaze powder is obtained by grinding blaze rods. It is the main ingredient required to make a potion of strength. To get blaze rods, you will need to visit the Nether and kill some Blaze mobs.

2. Fermented Spider Eye

Fermented Spider eye is a corrupting ingredient that can be used to change the effects of some potions. For instance, it can be distilled into potions of swiftness to convert them into potions of slowness. It can be crafted using a spider eye and sugar.

3. Netherwart

Netherwarts are often found growing in the Nether on patches of soul sand. You can harvest them and then easily farm them in the over world. All you need to do is get a few blocks of soul sand and plant the Netherwart seeds on those blocks.

Netherwart is a very important ingredient because it is used to make Awkward Potion which is the base for pretty much all the other potions.

4. Ghast Tear

Ghast tears are rare drops that you get when you kill a Ghast. They are really hard to get because Ghasts usually fly in unreachable places and can die over lava pools, which means the tear will be lost before you can collect it. Ghast tears are used to brew potion of regeneration.

5. Glistening Melon

Glistening melon can be crafted using eight gold nuggets and a slice of melon. It is used to brew potions of healing.

6. Glowstone Dust

Glowstone dust is an add-on ingredient that works as a potion modifier. It can be distilled into any potion to intensify the base effect of the potion. For instance, when distilled into a potion of strength, it increases the amount of strength boost the potion bestows. It can be obtained by breaking glowstone blocks.

7. Golden Carrot

Golden carrots are used to brew potions of night vision. They can be obtained using gold nuggets and a carrot.

8. Gunpowder

Gunpowder acts as a potion modifier ingredient. It can be distilled into any potion to turn the potion into a splash version of the base potion. Once a potion turns into a splash potion, the shape of the bottle changes. Also keep in mind that splash potion bottles cannot be reused unlike regular potion bottles and that splash potions usually have slightly weaker or shorter last effects than their drinkable versions.

It is excellent for distilling into harmful potions and using them as thrown weapons.

9. Magma Cream

Magma cream is obtained by killing magma cubes but can also be crafted using slime and blaze powder. It is used to brew potions of fire resistance.

10. Puffer Fish

These can be obtained occasionally by fishing. They are used to craft potions of water breathing. Keep in mind that you have a higher chance of catching something if you fish while it is raining.

11. Redstone Dust

Redstone dust acts as a potion modifier ingredient, same as glowstone dust. The difference is that in place of intensifying the effect of the potion it is distilled in to, redstone dust lengthens the effect. For example, if it is distilled into a potion of swiftness that lasts three minutes, afterward the potion will last nine minutes.

12. Spider Eye

Spider eye is dropped by spiders when they die. It can be used to brew potion of poison. It is also required to craft fermented spider eye.

13. Sugar

Obtained from sugarcane stalks. Sugar is used to brew potion of swiftness.

Potions

This section contains all the useful potions found in Minecraft, the ingredients required to brew them and details on how to brew them.

Awkward Potion

Acts as the base of almost every useful potion in the game. Keeping a stock of of these ready in a separate trunk is a good policy and saves time.

Ingredients

1. Water Bottle
2. Netherwart

Water Bottle + 🟤 ------> Awkward Potion

Potion of Swiftness

Increases movement speed by twenty percent and widens the field of view of whatever player it is used on. Lasts for three minutes in default form. Can be converted into potions of Swiftness II by distilling glowstone dust in it which makes it give a forty percent bonus to speed. Can be made to last for eight minutes instead of three by distilling redstone dust in it.

Useful for day to day uses as it saves time by making you go faster.

Ingredients

1. Awkward Potion
2. Sugar

Awkward Potion + ◇ ------> Potion of Swiftness

Potion of Strength

Increases the melee damage dealt by one hundred and thirty percent. Good potion for brawler type players. Lasts for one minute and thirty seconds in default form. Can be converted into potion of Strength II by distilling glowstone dust in it, which increases the bonus to two hundred and sixty percent. Redstone dust can be distilled into it to make it last for eight minutes.

Ingredients

1. Awkward Potion
2. Blaze Powder

Awkward Potion +  ------> Potion of Strength

Potion of Healing

Instantly restores two hearts of Health. Can be converted into potion of Healing II by distilling glowstone dust in it. This increase the number of hearts restored to four. Deals damage to undead like Zombies and skeletons.

Ingredients

1. Awkward Potion
2. Glistering Melon

Awkward Potion +  ------> Potion of Healing

Potion of Regeneration

Restores nine hearts of Health over a period of forty five second. Can be converted into its more potent form which restores nine hearts within twenty two seconds by distilling glowstone dust into it. Can be made to last for two minutes by distilling redstone dust in it.

Ingredients

1. Awkward Potion
2. Ghast Tear

Awkward Potion + ◊ -----> Potion of Regeneration

Potion of Fire Resistance

Makes the player immune to all fire damage, including ranged Blaze attacks and lava (allowing you to go for a very hot swim, ill advised as that might be). Lasts for three minutes in default form. Redstone dust can be distilled in it to make it last for eight minutes.

Ingredients

1. Awkward Potion

2. Magma Cream

Awkward Potion + ------> Potion of Fire Resistance

Potion of Night Vision

Brightens your sight so that even the darkest area can be seen clearly. Lasts for three minutes in default form but redstone dust can be distilled in it to make it last for eight minutes.

Ingredients

1. Awkward Potion

2. Golden Carrot

Awkward Potion + ------> Potion of Night Vision

Potion of Invisibility

As the name suggests, this potion makes you invisible, causing all hostile mobs turn neutral. Reloading chunks is sometimes required for mobs to stop attacking you. Lasts for three minutes in its default form. Redstone dust can be distilled in it to make it last for eight minutes.

Ingredients

1. Potion of Night Vision
2. Fermented Spider Eye

Potion of Night Vision + ⬤ ------> Potion of Invisibility

Potion of Water Breathing

Allows you to breath underwater. Lasts for three minutes but redstone dust can be distilled in it to make it last for eight minutes.

Ingredients

1. Awkward Potion
2. Pufferfish

Awkward Potion + ------> Potion of Water Breathing

Potion of Weakness

Lowers melee damage dealt by the affected entity by point five. Best used in splash form unless you want to drink it yourself. In splash form, it lasts for a little over a minute by default but redstone dust can be distilled in it to make it last for three minutes.

Ingredients

1. Awkward Potion
2. Fermented Spider Eye

Awkward Potion + ------> Potion of Weakness

Potion of Poison

Deals up to eighteen hearts worth of damage but does not reduce health value below half heart. It is the polar opposite of potion of regeneration and similar to it, it can be distilled with glowstone powder and redstone dust to change its effect intensity and time period.

Ingredients

1. Awkward Potion
2. Spider Eye

Awkward Potion + 🦑 ------> Potion of Poison

Potion of Slowness

Decreases the movement speed of the affected entity by fifteen percent. Lasts for a minute and thirty seconds in default form but can be distilled with redstone dust to make it last for four minutes.

Ingredients

1. Potion of Swiftness

2. Fermented Spider Eye

Potion of Swiftness + 🦠 -----> Potion of Slowness

Potion of Harming

Polar opposite of potion of healing. Does three hearts worth of damage in default form but effect can be intensified by distilling it with glowstone dust. Heals undead like Zombies and Skeletons.

Ingredients

1. Potion of Poison/Potion of Healing

2. Fermented Spider Eye

Potion of Poison / Healing + 🦠 -----> Potion of Harming

Enchanting

As mentioned earlier, enchantments are very useful and certain enchantments can give you powerful bonuses that give you a definite edge during game play.

To begin with enchanting, the first thing you need is an Enchanting Table. You can craft it using four blocks of obsidian, two diamonds and a book.

Once you have the table ready, you need to place it on a solid block to be able to use it. The best option is to make a separate enchanting room in your base.

Enchanting works using your experience. Experience can be collected by various activities in game. It appears in the form of shining green balls that are dropped whenever you kill some mob or mine a block of ore.

The following activities all grant different amounts of experience:

- Smelting Ore
- Killing Mobs
- Mining Ore
- Trading with Villagers
- Fishing
- Breeding Animals

When you right click on an enchantment table, you see the enchantment interface. In the empty slot, you can place any item that is enchant-able.

As soon as you place the item, the three slots on the right are filled with three different enchanting options. Each option has a number at the bottom right corner. This is the level of that enchantment.

If you do not have the required level, the option will be greyed out.

The other number is the number of Lapis Lazuli you will need to be able to use that enchantment. This is a new feture added in the latest update.

The gibberish written in each option is actually the *Standard Galactic Alphabet*. A key is given in the image below.

Unfortunately, even if you use the key to meticulously decrypt the words, you will find that they do not relate to the enchantment you might get from that option at all. The reason being that the words come randomly.

Before the latest update, you could never know for certain what enchantment you were going to get. However, with the revamped system that uses Lapis Lazuli, you can now get a hint of the enchantment by hovering your mouse over it.

And there is more to it. You will notice that just placing an enchanting table and using it will not give you enchantment options above level five no matter how much experience you have.

To remedy this, you need bookshelves. This is the reason that it is better to keep a separate room for enchanting. You need fifteen bookshelves to get level thirty enchantments which is the highest level enchantment you can get. Back in the day, it used to be level fifty, before the level cap was reduced because of certain ultra powerful level fifty enchantments which were almost game breaking.

However, there are some upsides too. High level enchantments can have the chance of giving you multiple enchantments on your item in one go, so it is worth it to craft some books and bookshelves.

Another point of note is that you can also enchant books and save the enchantments to be used later. Enchanted books can be used with Anvils to transfer their enchantment onto a compatible item. More on this in the next section.

Enchanting and Anvils

Anvils are blocks that can be used to repair items, enchant them using enchanting books and combine two enchanted items into one item which has the effects of both its parent items. It can even be used to rename items.

All these activites cost experience points, depending on the level of enchantments and the equipment in question.

Anvils also deteriorate over time with every use and eventually get destroyed.

List of Enchantments

Below is a table with a list of all the enchantments you can find in game, with their corresponding effects and the items on which they can be applied.

Keep in mind that the higher the level of the enchantment, the better its effect and the more experience you will need to unlock the enchantment. For instance, Protection IV will give better bonus than Protection I but will also be costlier.

Enchantment Name	Maximum Level	Objects	Effect
Protection	IV	All armor	Reduces physical damage
Fire Protection	IV	All armor	Reduces fire damage and burn time, includes damage from lava
Blast Protection	IV	All armor	Reduces damage from explosions
Feather Falling	IV	Boots	Reduces fall damage
Projectile Protection	IV	All armor	Reduces damage from all projectiles
Thorns	III	All armor	Damages attackers based on enchantment level
Sharpness	V	Sword/ ax	Increases damage of item

Smite	V	Sword/ ax	Increases damage to undead mobs
Bane of Arthropods	V	Sword/ ax	Increases damage to spiders and silverfish
Knockback	II	Sword	Pushes mobs back when hit
Fire Aspect	II	Sword	Sets target mob on fire
Power	V	Bow	Increases damage done by arrows
Punch	II	Bow	Pushes target back
Flame	I	Bow	Arrows set mobs on fire
Infinity	I	Bow	One arrow can be used infinite times
Unbreaking	III	Most weapons tools and armor	Increases durability of tools, armor and weapons
Respiration	III	Helmet	Extends underwater breathing time and improves vision
Aqua Affinity	I	Helmet	Increases the speed of mining underwater
Depth Strider	III	Boots	Increases the horizontal swimming speed inside water
Looting	II	Sword	Increases the number of drops as well as the chance of rare mob drops

Efficiency	V	Tools	Increases the mining speed. Correct tools must be used with a block to get the boost
Silk Touch	I	Tools	Mined blocks drop themselves instead of dropping the usual items. (For instance mining ore block will drop ore block)
Fortune	III	Tools	Increases the number of items dropped by a mined block
Luck of the Sea	III	Fishing Rod	Reduces the chance of catching junk
Lure	III	Fishing Rod	Increases the rate at which fishes bite the hook

Conclusion

While enchanting is a bit of an iffy business what with all the randomness and chance, if you try long enough, you are bound to get the enchantment you want.

Potion making, on the other hand, depends on your capacity to decide as to what potion to use at a certain time. As long as you do not muddle up and use the best suited potion, you will find that all your encounters are a breeze.

Keep brewing and keep enchanting!

Happy Gaming!